Untethered: The Voices of the Unknown

Ashley Boyd

BookLeaf Publishing

India | USA | UK

Untethered: The Voices of the Unknown ©
2024 Ashley Boyd

Presentation by *BookLeaf Publishing*

Web: www.bookleafpub.com

E-mail: info@bookleafpub.com

ISBN: 9789363319554

First edition 2024

ACKNOWLEDGEMENT

I would like to acknowledge myself. For my ability to keep going, for never giving up, for finding solace in my writing when life didn't make sense. I would also like to acknowledge my mother for holding space for my growth that has allowed me to be where I am at this very moment. I would also like to acknowledge my ancestors. For their support, their love, their continuous guidance in moments of confusion. I would not be who I am without them, and I would not be here without the spiritual connection of my mother offering herself as a vessel for me to come earthside and experience what it means to be human.

PREFACE

I would like to start by saying this journey is not an easy one; there are no quick fixes, shortcuts, or cheat codes. We are all discovering, learning, and unlearning what this "inbetween" means. What it means to be whole in the space of void. What it's like to finally hear those "unknown" voices and give them the love and acknowledgment that they need. Embrace and love every part of you, as it once was a voice that may not have been heard.

God's Gift

Cheekbones ascended, where the Angel rested
their gaze.
A light that shines so brightly that it outshines
the fire's brilliant haze.
Your body dances through the flame as the
Phoenix rises.
The way your wrap sits upon your head, as
though God placed his arms ever so gently
around your crown himself.
Your voice sings so melodically with every word
you speak.
Every vowel, sentence, every syllable sounds
like the glimmer of 1000 fairies.
The way your essence falls onto the presence of
those you bless,

It is that of a lingering perfume, even after you have left.
Skin as soft as cocoa butter, but as pure as crack in its raw form.
A drug, similar to the high you get off life when your spirit is aligned with that of the unknown.
You see, you are beauty in its rarest form.
The fountain of youth that all search for but never find.
As the everlasting love is something that lives within.
It's in you, not on you. Not something you can easily find.
A sense of grace that cannot be packaged and sold in stores.
Its quality is something that cannot be replicated.
Clothed in God's eternal beauty lies a forbidden Goddess that many may wonder but will not seek.
For you are cloaked in God's blessing, in God's beauty, in God's salvation.
Only those who have never experienced an energy so pure will come by hundreds, thousands, of souls, racing.

Mystery

I want you to fill me up
Fuck me
Suck me
Kiss me
Squeeze me
Enter my soul as I welcome you with open arms
My body rises to the occasion
Let this devilish look in my eyes be the
persuasion
Perspiration falls as our souls crash together like
giant waterfalls
Hitting the rocks

Water beating down on my skin
You fill my stomach with passion
Igniting a fire within.
Allowing my soul to be set free
Bells are ringing, my moan keeps singing, my
body rises as my freedom keeps ringing.
Rising to the occasion, your lips being the
persuasion, telling me to come along.
A journey filled with glitter and gold, our bodies
explode as our juices flow like an ancient river.
My river runs downstream, my juices turn into
cream; you drink me up like the fountain of
youth, with every lick, ice cream.
Filling your soul with my liquid gold, you
would've sworn this was a fantasy. I want you to
Fuck me
Suck me
Kiss me
Squeeze me
Fill me with your wildest dreams.

Thief

We're so worried about having the next Ring
Doorbell,
the highest tech security system, even the
biggest dog to ensure we're safe.
But we rob ourselves every day.
We rob ourselves of joy every time we hold onto
emotions that are meant to stay in motion.
We rob ourselves every time we chain ourselves
down when an opportunity presents itself for us
to grow.
We rob ourselves every time we say yes when
we really want to say no.
We rob ourselves every time we know "this is
the last time" should've been the last damn time.

We rob ourselves every time we know we need
time to ourselves but so freely give that to
others.
You see, we speak so highly of how the
government bends us over and takes what little
dignity we have left…
Yet and still, we bend ourselves over every day,
Compromising what morals, values, and
boundaries we have left.
So yes, every 1 out of 3 people DO get robbed
every day.
Robbed of joy, happiness, sanity, creation,
wealth, abundance, and peace.
You see if we viewed these things as
transactions on our bank account
Who would we call when things are in the
negative?
Would we find a way to report our
transgressions and find a
quick and easy way to file a claim for the very
things we have chosen to take?
What use is it to cry over spilled milk,
When you know… you know you're just going
to keep leaving it on the edge with the top off?
You see, we can't keep expecting people to rally
in rage over the same choices we choose to
make.

Soon, there will come a time when we are tired
of going into our wallets to pay for an
experience we can no longer afford.
Because now you've gone bankrupt to pay for
things that hold no value.

"Dear Diary"

January 16, 2024

12:27 a.m.

My goal for 2024 is to be here. By that, I don't just mean physically; I mean mentally. You see, 2023 turned me into a zombie. Allowing myself to be consumed by various things, sadness, depression, and pain. My goal is to be here. To inhale more of the good shit and exhale the bullshit. To allow the sun to penetrate my skin, allowing me to sink into my body rather than fighting to swim. My goal is to be here. To not allow society's bodily standards from enjoying this vessel that God gave me. To wear fancy

clothes just because it's Tuesday, simply because
I have forgotten what my body looks like
without sweatpants and a T-shirt. My goal is to
be here. To allow my face to be the canvas of all
the creations begging to be made. To feel like I
can create someone new each day. This is my
vessel, right? So I can adorn it as I please.
Whether that is doing makeup or putting on my
jewelry. My goal is to be here. To be the mom
that my son deserves without allowing
overstimulation or finances to get in the way of a
life that I have earned. To allow my inner child
to play with my son relentlessly, to show my son
life doesn't always have to be so serious, and
mommy doesn't have to be so mean. My goal is
to be here. To realize I am more than my
emotions, and I don't have to dance with the
fantasies of death. Dancing with the idea that my
existence is no longer needed, as I scream and
shout from under the rubble of my emotions that
have impeded me. The weight of emotions
crushing my chest, making me feel as though the
only way to cope is to flirt with death. Feeling
the pressure ease off of me as I immerse myself
in the worlds that are simply educational fiction.
You know the media, where not everyone wants
to be social. They just want to use entertainment
as an escape from their own pain. While
scrolling on by as though they are walking down

the streets like zombies, refusing to
acknowledge the mere existence of the humans
that are around them. When really it's just an
excuse, to excuse their own pain, while
meddling in their fantasies. My goal is to be
here. To feel the love I have dreamt of, to taste
the foods my body has denied for years, to hear
the sound of my heartbeat going at a steady pace
because anxiety and depression no longer
cripple me, to feel my feet touch the ground of a
life I don't have to run from, to smell fresh rain,
as I am no longer allowing my fears to keep me
held hostage in my own brain. My goal is to
feel, to be, to embrace, to savor each moment
that 2024 has to offer me.

Canvas

I want you to hear me… the whispers of the
wind, the sounds of the birds chirping as I paint
the sky while the sun rises
I want you to hear me… the unspoken words
Exchanged between two minds coming together
as one something close to the divine.
I want you to hear me… the leaves chasing one
another with no final destination as to where
they will go.
Red, gold, green, and yellow dancing through
the streams, painting a perfect picture that we
have yet to see.
I want you to hear me, to allow your senses to
take you on a ride, with me the divine, to the
places where no one knows.
Where the mysteries of life have yet to unfold.

Gentle

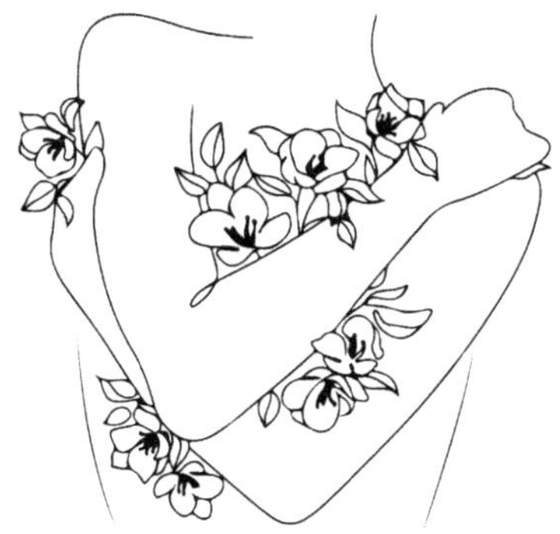

Being gentle with yourself feels like,
The cold side of the pillow on a hot summer
night.
Being gentle with yourself feels like,
Laughing when you push a pull door.
Being gentle with yourself feels like,
When you spill water on the floor…
And instead of insulting yourself, you say, "it's
okay, we can clean it up."
Being gentle with yourself feels like,
That long-awaited cry,
When someone asks, "are you okay?"
Being gentle with yourself feels like,
Seeing who you used to be without judgment,
but knowing they did their very best.
Being gentle with yourself feels like,

Relaxed shoulders, an unclenched jaw, and
relaxed fists.
Being gentle with yourself feels like,
God giving you a second chance to love your
inner child unconditionally.
Being gentle with yourself means,
You no longer feel like an outsider.
Simply because you don't strive to fit in.
Being gentle with yourself looks like,
Being comfortable in your outfit…
Without feeling like you have to keep adjusting
it, just so that you don't bring too much
attention.
Being gentle with yourself sounds like,
Speaking to yourself positively out loud
As your nervous system relaxes, knowing you're
safe from harm.
Being gentle with yourself tastes like that last
spoonful of ice cream after a hard day,
Even when you know you're over your calorie
count.
Being gentle with yourself smells like,
Knowing that a pile of clothes can't stand to sit
another day… but instead, you show gratitude
for having the means to clean them.
Being gentle with yourself looks a lot like,
The things we don't see,
hear,
or speak often.

But these love songs remain unsung in our
hearts.
For the words that merely bring us a sense of
peace,
Yet not be uttered out loud.
It is our body that feels the peace that washes
over us like a warm shower, melting away the
day.
Knowing,
If at first we don't succeed…
There's always room tomorrow to try again.

Self Pleasure

When it comes to masturbation, it feels like it's
become a lost art.
Living in a world where all these toys help us to
fuck ourselves as hard as the men that carelessly
broke our hearts.
Which toy can make us cum the quickest?
Which toy can feel like the real thing?
There is a lost art in knowing the moment you
touch yourself, your whole body melts as though
it's been waiting for your touch.
Feening for this moment, you realize your body
has been craving you. Parting your lips, you feel
your pussy pulsating as though she knows she's
going to be touched.
Placing one finger inside yourself just to see
how that feels. Gripping your fingers like it's got
a secret to tell.
A shiver goes up your spine as you feel the
warmth of the wetness on your hand.
Taking the time to hear the sounds of your
juices, slowly bringing your hand back up to
taste yourself.

Circling your fingers over your clit, tracing your
wetness like an old story.
There's a lost art in fingering yourself, figuring
out how many fingers inside feel the best.
Choosing the pace at which you want to circle
back over your clit.
Fingering yourself with one hand and playing
with your clit with the other. Switching
positions, moving even faster, toes curling as
you feel everything build up inside of you.
Moving your hand away to catch your breath.
Edging yourself to allow the intensity to build.
Then doing it again, and again, and again
Until your fingers are soaking wet, then you hear
that voice in the back of your mind saying, "cum
for me."
Your breathing picks up the faster you move,
your body rising and falling with each surge that
passes through you.
As soon as you feel your hand soak, "your body
begins to sink beneath the surface as it relaxes
from the buildup of intensity."
Your hand, still sitting in its wetness as you
slowly fall into a deep sleep.
An experience no toy can bring.

8 of Swords

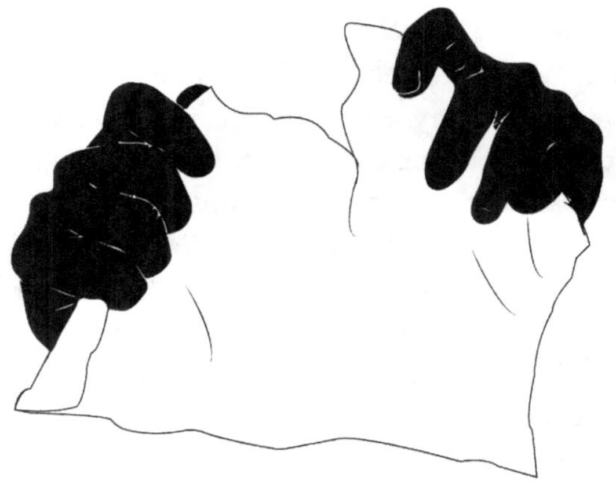

A part of me feels that when I separated myself from the world, my heart spilt open. The contents of my addictions spilling over onto my hard work. Codependency, social media, comparing, and emptiness. Hitting the table like an empty bottle of alcohol. I sit there and stare as I've drowned out the things I do not talk about. Only to end up over the toilet the next morning staring at the very things I suppressed. Low self-esteem, imposter syndrome, insecurity, and the sense of longing to be seen. Laying on the toilet, holding onto what last bit of hope I have left. I muster the strength to pick myself up again, only to find myself taking a shot of liquid courage in hopes it will help me believe in myself again. Drunken off my own lies as I sit there lifeless, waiting for the next bump to hit me. Waiting to feel that same high I did back in 2020. Chasing a feeling that was tied to overworking myself for less than I am worth. Being surrounded by people who only loved me for what I created, not who I was as a person. You see, it's easy to snatch the cloth off the table when your favorite idol shows you they too are still human. It's easy to shatter the reality of false hopes you have molded this person to be. Only to see your fantasy go up in flames. You weren't in love with me, only who I claimed to be. You saw only a mirror reflection of yourself, slowly realizing I too was just as broken as you. You tiptoe over the glass shards, hoping that maybe if you don't look down, you can't see. I was simply reflecting back to you what you saw in me.

11:11

The moments of adversity where I fight back
from allowing you into my space.
The place where I lay my heart… I mean my
head.
Thoughts running rampantly as I inhale your
scent. Do I stay where I am?
Or do I go?
Is this a place that's safe for me to call home?
If I tell you all my secrets, will you run and
throw away the key?
Or hold them as close to your heart in the same
way you do me?

Can I trust you to hold my fears? To know that
even when life comes crashing down, you're the
only one who won't disappear.
You see, I'm afraid for a love like this to
swallow me whole.
In the same way, a giant ship gets sucked into
the abyss.
Lost at sea, or is it lost at see?
Blinded by a love I can't see.
I can only feel you, taste you, touch you, smell
you. As a means to know this isn't a facade.
A love so beautifully packaged,
and sent to me… it could've only been delivered
by God.
With such patience, love, compassion, and
grace.
A love that I no longer desire to escape. For this
is the space I return to when I know I'm not
well. As I bury my face into your chest, soaking
them with the tears enough to fill a wishing well.
By the time I have dried my face, all the things
I've wished for no longer seem to be far away.
Dried eyes, no longer comforted by soothing
lies, I no longer choose to hide. From the lust,
the pain, the fears, and frustrations that
tomorrow may bring.
No matter what I carry into this new day,
I know when it comes to loving you, this love I
prayed for is here to stay…

Conquer

You aren't in competition with anyone but
yourself.
The writings left on the walls by your past,
are simply a present left so you can move
forward with grace.
Utilize the stories of yesterday… to simply be a
guide for where you're headed.
Tell yourself thank you. For enduring what you
couldn't today.
So that you can move without fear, conquer any
obstacles placed in front of you.
The tools left in the darkened corner. There for
you to maneuver through high waters
effortlessly.

So for today, and today only. You are not in
competition with yourself. But in union.
For it is who you were yesterday that carries you
into who you are today.

Comfort

The weight that sits in my hands doesn't feel
like a burden to carry.
More like a weighted blanket that lays on my
mind, helping to keep my thoughts grounded as
it's taken for a ride.
The feeling of the pages as I excitedly turn,
wondering what awaits me.
Eager to see what my imagination has crafted on
this blank canvas.
The smell as I open it each time, knowing this
next journey will be different from the last.

Sitting there as the sun hits my skin while I
nuzzle deeper into my blanket, getting lost in the
pages.
With each turn, it's like white noise, shutting out
any ounce of the outside world as I bury myself
in a different reality.
Hoping if I go deep enough, I'll find something
I've been longing for.
Although, these moments must come to an end
as my skin is kissed by the light of the moon.
Telling me it's time to end my adventure for the
day.
There will always be tomorrow—a new day, a
new page, a new adventure to explore.

Runneth Dry

It was me… I did it
I sat there with a delighted smile
Pouring into your cup
Making sure no matter what your cup was
always filled
The cracks in my lips
Clearing my throat as I wince at the pain of it
catching from the dryness.
Instead, I allowed myself to be filled with
rage, envy, hate, and sadness.
Each time I heard, "are you okay?"
I fought to crack a smile as my lips bled from
dehydration…
I replied, I'm doing fine, how are you?
Knowing that I needed to say…

I'm falling apart while fighting to keep myself
together.
I need a hug so tight that at least my cup will be
filled with my tears.
So that maybe I can use them to wash away the
pain I may feel.
Using those tears to clear away any fatigue I
have carried for so long.
So that I have the strength to tell myself… no.
We will not pour into anyone else's cup when
our own is bone dry.
We will not go out of our way to make sure
someone else is filled with love, so that they
may not feel an ounce of what we do.
We will not allow our cup to runneth dry while
pouring whatever is left from our reservoir…
Even if it means sparing only the few drops left
to get us by.
I will not sit and painfully crack a smile, as the
blood from my lips drips and mixes with the
tears falling from my eyes.
It was me, I did it. I chose to water myself with
the tears that filled my cup.

Siren

I never knew what it meant when it was spoken
Hell hath no fury, like a woman scorned.
You see, a woman's heart and love are
immeasurable.
But she can only take so much.
The lies that you bury in the backyard of your
home,
are only the fertilizer for the breeding grounds of
a woman who hath yet been scorned?
The very taste of deceit that lies upon your lips
Is only a matter of time before that sweet flavor,
soon tastes sour.

The taste will begin to settle as she ponders
what's changed.
She will swallow every last drop until one day,
Her spirit will recognize it is not what she
remembers.
The sweet love that once graced her lips, is no
longer sealed with a kiss.
It now lays upon her cheek, in hopes she may
not realize this love is no longer sweet.
Each day she will see what once gratuitously
poured into her cup runs dry.
That gentle caress of your hands as they run
down the back of her spine.
It's the subtle graze of a kiss from your lips
That allows the lies and deceit to convince her
you'll be running late for dinner.
It is the curiosity that wraps its arms around her
cold body as she lies in bed waiting for you.
It is curiosity that holds her hand as it leads her
to the attic, rummaging through her mind as she
runs to old photo boxes…
Searching for the answers to her questions that
lie dormant in the back of her mind.
Like the untouched wedding dress, she's kept to
remind her of the day everything in her life
made sense.
She sits there as the dust collects at her feet,
tears welling up in her eyes.

The man she loved, the heart whom she shared a
home with, was no longer hers… and hers only.
Hell hath no fury like a woman scorned.
She chuckles as the scent of dinner lingers…
trailing behind it is the scent of the woman.
A scent of sweetness, unfamiliar but alluring.
Staring into her husband's eyes,
seeing that a new imprint has been made on his
soul.
A smile you haven't seen since you held your
wedding pictures so tightly in your hand.
"How was your day, honey? It was great!"
Is that where it ends?
What was once a space to share the details is
filled with silence to avoid anything that could
unveil the source of the sweet scent that lingers
on your clothes…
Each time you pass by, the scent fills me up.
Only to be met with a pain in the pit of my
stomach, knowing it's not my own.
So when the happiness turns into pain, and pain
into fury, I want you to know it was the sweet
scent that you carried home.
It was the taste of your lies that eventually
settled into my stomach
The deceit you planted in my mind led me to
believe home was no longer where the heart is.

For this woman hath no fury, only a wounded
soul by the one who vowed to guard it from the
secrets of the unknown.
For I should've known, hell hath no fury like a
woman scorned.

Sin

What you don't face, your children will.
Maybe not today, tomorrow, or next week.
It'll be the moments when life gives them
everything it has to offer.
Only for what seems like a minor
inconvenience,
To later on echo in their minds, reminding them
of who they never wanted to be.
It's that moment
when your daughter gazes into the mirror,
a whispered sigh escapes her lips as she notices
the gentle curve of cellulite.
It's that moment when your son
utters the word "bitch" as he smells the scent

Of his crush's favorite perfume being carried
away as she giggles at his propose.
It's that moment when your daughter's best
friend squeals,
As she gets that cute purse she's always wanted,
but she fights back tears, knowing she can't
afford it.
It's that moment your son goes to cry, only to be
met with your cold demeanor and disgust as you
tell him to toughen up.
It's never the first, second, third, or 17th time
that it finally sticks.
It's those moments, THEY, least expect it.
It's the moment they're going to a party and that
one hair is out of place, the dress is too tight, or
their teeth aren't straight enough.
It's the moments their self-esteem can't carry
them through the pain.
So they seek solace in the words they heard you
utter.
I hate my hair, I wish I was skinnier, I wish I had
a better smile.
Hearing these things rings a sense of familiarity.
The words crush you. The realization of the
poison you forced yourself to drink,
and left on the bathroom counter was consumed
by your child, not realizing what it was.
There was no

"Warning, be careful to keep away from children" sign on this bottle left at the prying hands of a curious child.
A child who wondered why no matter how much love, how much hairspray, how many outfit changes later… their parents did not seem to love themselves.
So this is love? Ummhmmm?
The question that replayed like a somber song, only to be met by the melodies of horror.
How could something placed in a beautiful bottle contain something so dangerous?
The makeup, the hairspray, the grim smile, the tough boy act was simply a wolf in sheep's clothing.
Hoping and yearning if the disguise blended in good enough, they would be as confident as the sheep they surrounded themselves with.
Only to see… the sheep's fur was tended with love.
The peace they radiated was by the hand of the sun, making sure to melt their stresses away.
The love they had was simply accepting who they are is okay. I don't strive to be any other sheep but me.
If I wasn't meant to be this way, God wouldn't have crafted me so perfectly.
That piece of hair? Merely an opportunity to try out a different hairstyle!

That dress? Maybe it's time I broke out that old sewing machine I've been meaning to dust off! That crooked smile? These teeth are only temporary. Soon enough, I'll have a new set! Sometimes the imperfections are God's lesson to love yourself as you are, sometimes a little bit more.

So for today, love yourself a little bit more.
Look at yourself a little bit more loving.
Speak a little bit nicer to yourself.

1:11

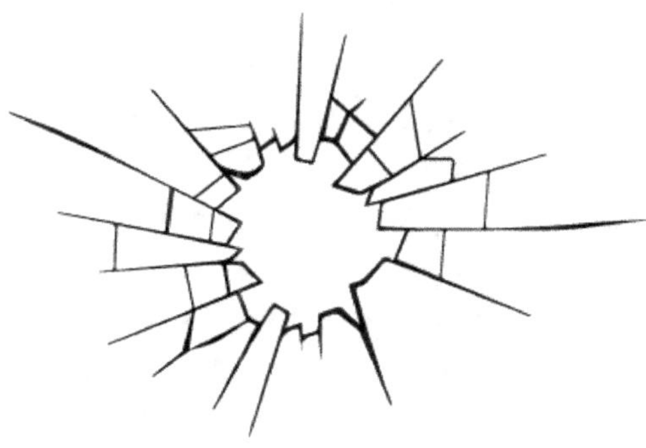

You see, me leaving you alone isn't just for
you…
Or for me.
It's for the sake of the weight you put on my
spirit,
For the sake of these burdens, I refuse to carry.
The burdens of your past in which you refuse to
let go.
For the sake of you not finding a home within
my soul,
To lay your head down as a means of an escape,
from a god-awful place you can't even stand the
sight of.
A means of a way to disqualify yourself from
running this race.
A means of a way to catch your breath from
trying to escape the troubles of your past.

Only expecting me to be your saving Grace.
You see, me leaving you alone isn't just for you
or for me.
It's for my ancestors who have fought day in and
day out to give me the strength to see another
day.
For they know my will to live isn't as willing,
As I have no saving grace.
If I fall from my own good graces,
I am left to pick up the pieces and rediscover
A whole new meaning of what true love is.
Not to be Frank, or even to be true.
You see, me leaving things alone was never for
me; it was for you.
To avoid the catastrophe of holding onto this
spoiled milk longer than intended.
But it's better to hold onto it than to cry over it,
right?
There's no sense in crying over what isn't mine.
What God has intended for me will always show
its light.
Through my darkest days, at the end of every
tunnel,
as a means of a breakthrough from the obstacles
that only took me to another dark place.
So that I could see the light and realize…
You see, me leaving you alone was never for
you; it was for me.

Silence

I remember the words like they were said
yesterday: you hate your child, your ancestors
hate you.
You see, it was in that moment of silence, those
words I thought I erased were gone.
It was in silence I noticed the lingering ink stains
from trying to erase the words that lie dormant
in my mind.
It was in this moment of silence I truly started to
understand how mental health works.
It is not just how you treat someone, but what
you say to them.
The ugly thoughts that run through your head as
you itch to find somewhere to get rid of them.
So you throw stones at what you thought was
your enemy's glass house. Only to realize it was
just a mirror of the things you refused to see.
Seeing your illusions shatter right in front of you
as you try to grasp reality without leaving a trace
of the stones you cast.

Hiding your bloody hands.
They say sticks and stones may break my bones,
But words cannot hurt me.
So why do the words you cast cut just as deep as
the stones you threw?
Why not once did you stop to see the fog on the
glass as you screamed the things you felt about
yourself to me?
Making me the main character in your story that
you refuse to read.
Inserting your own improvisations to fit the
narrative you've created.
Don't you think the same person who advocates
for suicide awareness shouldn't cast stones at
those because you too refuse to accept the fact
you don't want to be here either?
Or was that a lie too? Words you etched into
your own mind now nobody can take the pen
you used and erase these new lines you've
written into your own story.
Maybe it's time to redefine what mental health
looks like to you…
Maybe next time the pen you'll use in your own
story will be red instead of blue.

10:23

I'm not talking about the mess you have to clean
up after the chaos has ensued in your heart.
I'm talking about the mess,
The mess a child makes as the various colors of
paint ooze between their fingers
As it captivates their senses, filling their hearts
with glee.
I'm talking about the mess
The mess that takes place
when the goosebumps rise on your skin from
playing with your siblings throwing ice-cold
water at each other.
Make a mess,
The mess a child makes at 4 am as they steadily
pour milk into the bowl before the cereal

Just so that they can spill it all over the floor as
they carry it to their parents' room.
Make a mess today,
Stand in front of the mirror because
Today you chose to say fuck depression and
skew your makeup brushes across the counter
As you paint the walls of your heart with your
favorite colors
As you spray the setting spray to set your
intentions for the day.
"I will not allow depression to claim my days
anymore."
Make a mess today.
The kind that leaves everlasting memories,
forever etched into your heart
Stories told, 1000 years old, by the ancestors
Old folklore, they'd call it.
Make a mess today.

Double Stuf Standards

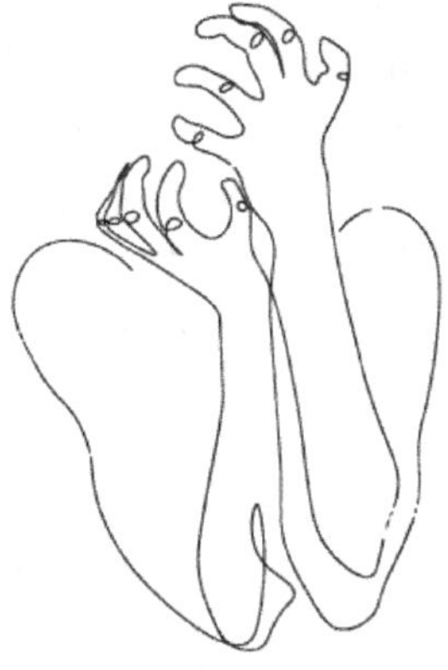

To say that every man ain't shit is a lie you tell
yourself to comfort you from the blood-stained
wounds that linger like the old memories you
can't seem to run from.
To stumble and realize you're projecting every
man to be just like your father, your ex, your
uncle, your brother.
To say every man ain't shit would mean…
After you leave your dusty ass ex alone,
Every man you encounter is an alcoholic just
because you sat from across the bar admiring the
way his eyes glimmer from the light;
while simultaneously counting how many beers
he had that night.
To say every man ain't shit would mean,

As you sit at the round table, you admire the guy
across from you and his tattoos.
While noticing he's on his 3rd blunt,
As you replay the memories of the last ex who
begged you for another $50 to cover his half of
the rent because he'd rather escape his problems
than keep a roof over your head.
To say every man ain't shit would mean…
This next guy that you're so madly in love with
can't stay off his phone because it must mean
he's cheating.
But every given chance you've had to take a
journey into his world as a graphic designer, you
decline.
It's easier to assume it must be someone else,
Even though he fights to share that part of
himself with you.
It's easier to push away every man that even
seems to get close to you.
Just because making an excuse for every man
that even so resembles the ones that hurt you is
easier than digging into a part of yourself that
holds this pain so close to you.
As close as the teddy bear you held,
During the moments, your father came home
high.
The moments your mom had to work 3 jobs just
to cover rent.

The times that your dad would come home late smirking as he gazed into his phone with bloodshot eyes and the subtle scent of a perfume that was not your mother's.
It's easier to blame every man who even remotely seems to resemble your father while shining light on the wounds you have yet to heal…
But just take this moment to smile.
To know, as much as it hurts to close a chapter of your life, you so badly wanted to have a happy ending to–
You chose to put yourself first and left every time. Each time you could've stayed where you were enduring the same pain as your mother,
Crying yourself to sleep over the sins of your father.
You let each tear you shed be the first and the last.
As you'd rather wipe them away from laughing so hard than feel the tightness in your chest wondering what, where you went wrong.
So take this time to admire your strength, courage, and resiliency.
That smile is the best asset to make up your true beauty.

Wild Fire

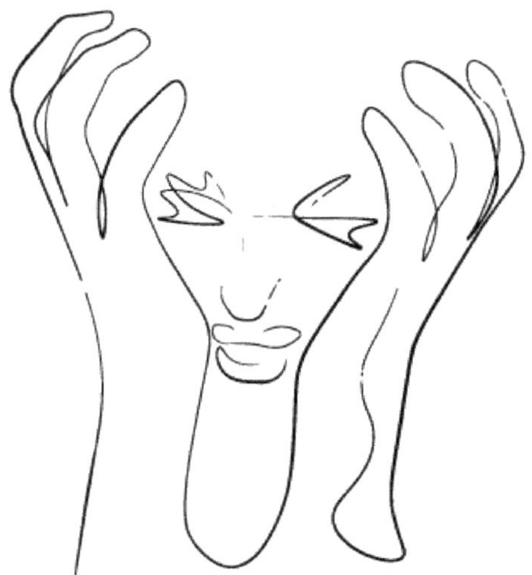

Save me from thy wrath that be mine own rage
As my words spew, setting ablaze the fire that
burns the bridge beneath me
The wood I carried now seeps into my soul
Using now what was the bridge I burnt, to build
a place called home.
The key that now unlocks the door.

The piece of you, you left behind found its way
into my locket that sits on my chest where your
curly strands used to lay.

Your thoughts caught in between each curl,
tangled, dancing to the beat of my heart as it
sings the song of the ancient times.
For the flowers that sit in your eyes grow just as
wide as your smile as the sun spreads to lay a
kiss upon your cheek… revealing your golden
skin, as I run my fingers across and sink down
just as the
way in which my feet bury into the sand to leave
an imprint that says
"Your heart is a place I call home; with the lock
and key in tow, may the rain cover the trees that
provide the shade just as those beautiful eyes set
ablaze to the fire that burns within my heart."
Was that too much? A trail that goes into the
mountains just to show where our love story
starts… or maybe it was never enough. I can
only hope, the wood that has seeped into my
heart is enough to keep us warm on our coldest
days.
Cause even though the growth it provides, I
can't seem to stand the rain.

Sky Miles: 1,111 Miles

Just as you're about to take flight, you notice a
letter sitting up under your seat.
You reach to see, and you're met with the words,
"To my future self."
You're about to take a flight back home,
But not the place you grew up in,
The place where you lost the pieces of the
puzzle to make you whole.
You'll find things you didn't know about
yourself; you'll see things you didn't know were
there.
As you walk through the door, you come across
this lamp in the corner.
The closer you get, the louder the buzzing gets.

You step closer, proceeding with caution, you
see the Bulb says "A11, Watt 460."
You notice how the light bulb hasn't been
changed since 1998.
Bringing your hand towards it, you notice it's
cold.
Searching around the room for a new one, you
see this beautiful Golden Case that reads…
"Open As Needed." But is it time?
How long has this light started to fade?
Until you hear "You're Ready."
You find a hammer nearby, proceeding to smash
the case. The thought of this new reality, cutting
your hands and falling at your feet, you ask
again, "am I ready?"
Stepping forward little by little, wincing, crying,
feeling each shard of glass piercing through your
skin, you reach for the bulb.
You can either sit to tend to your wounds,
Or put one foot in front of the other to change,
make the change.
Deciding the darkness was enough, you go to
remove the bulb only to realize it's gone warm.
The more you try to unscrew it, the hotter it gets.
Pushing through, you carefully place the new
bulb in; despite being afraid of being burned
again, you still push through anyway.
First thing you notice is the buzzing sound is
gone; you can now hear the sound of leaves, the

wind blowing, you can finally hear yourself think.

It's not until then, you see all the paintings on the wall, the different color chalk smudges, you hear a faint laugh even.

You sit there wondering why you could never see all this before until you realized that light bulb was you.

The flickering light waiting to be noticed, the repetitive buzzing of options telling you what you should do, who you should be like.

Even down to the outdated bulb, why did nobody notice how dim your light was?

Why did no one notice every time you lit up, you second-guessed yourself?

Why did no one notice the outdated beliefs you carried so close to your heart that were never even yours to carry?

Why did no one notice that maybe you just needed to change? To be updated? To be given the opportunity to allow that little girl to use her light in ways she never got a chance to?

So I want you to ask, am I willing to shine my brightest without worrying about someone dimming my light?

Power Balls

You know what I fucking hate? I hate when I'm playing a game and my special reward is 30 more minutes to fucking play. I don't want to play for 30 more minutes without losing any lives! I want more power-ups to pass this level I've been on for 3 weeks! You see, this shit reminds me a lot about life. You ask the universe to provide the resources to do what you need to, to level up in life. What does it do? Gives you more space and time to process your triggers. To sit in the same spot wondering what the fuck is wrong with me? Why do I feel like a level that no matter how strategic I am, I cannot beat it!?

Why does it feel like no matter how much I try to play for fun, it just ends up being a useless punching bag where I angrily tap the screen in hopes my next move will be the one to let me win this level. But wait! My finger slipped, and I only moved two pieces. Does life still reward you even if you only got 2 things moved off your to-do list of 106? Does life give you more time when it feels like you're failing? Does life give you rewards for every time you've worked hard to reach higher than the last? Does life allow you to go on little quests to keep yourself occupied from the thoughts that roam your mind, hoping to make the house of your heart a HOME?! Does life let you pause the game and come back months later because this shit is just too fucking much?! Does life allow you to buy more power-ups when it seems you can't even do something as simple as folding a load of clothes? I often wonder if life truly was like a game: would I fight to get to the next level or simply play for my enjoyment? 9:09.

Blind Lady

Blind lady, staring out the window, minding the
business that doesn't pay you. They say
Godliness is next to cleanliness, so why are you
not taking the time to wipe off your reflection in
order to see the man in the mirror. Opening your
closet, trying to see what facade you're going to
wear today. Skeletons pile up next to the laundry
you have yet to clean. It's time to clear out your
history and stop holding onto the baggage.
Carrying around the past in a plastic bag.
Hoping nobody judges you for your past, looks
at your bag, telling you to let it go; it's simply
trash. Why are you so aggressive? Let that hurt
go. Let those tears flow. Let go of what's not for

you. Wipe the fog away from your glasses to
see; you've graduated from the bag to the blind
lady. You've become someone even you don't
know. From bag to blind lady, leave your
problems at the door. For it was never meant for
you to find a new place to carry this baggage.
Just sit it down and walk away and open up to a
new path. One you cannot see, peeking through
a plastic bag, or bursting at the seams. Allow life
to show what it's been trying to offer you. It may
be old, it may be new, it may be borrowed, or
something blue. But you will never know until
you let go, step outside, and leave those
problems at the door.

Truth Is…

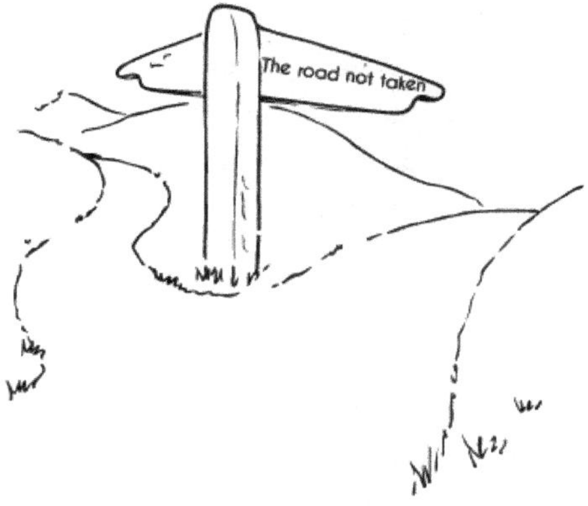

It may be time to realize on your end there was underlying competition. But there was also a mix of I have to know everything and be everything to everyone. Maybe the competition was because you felt you had to go at everyone else's pace and you took "maybe you should keep this in mind for later" as a means to do everything right now. Maybe you needed to separate to find yourself and realize the competition was and has only been you. Your want and need to always be better. Your want and need to make sure you never fail. You see, you never realized how critical your FOMO was until you had to walk away from the very thing that was supposed to give you the tools to

manage the eruption when it spilled into areas of
your life and burned the bridges you felt needed
to be saved. Maybe you needed to take a step
back so you could see you had a match lit ready
to throw at the very bridges you built. To see
that you would do anything to keep yourself
warm, even if that meant bringing harm to
others. Maybe this is why you needed to remove
yourself from everyone so that you could use
that match to set your soul on fire. So the
warmth you could feel could be due to the very
things that brought you joy. Maybe you needed
to learn to keep your light to yourself for a while
just so you could feel the very warmth that
draws people in. You will never see the light that
everyone else does if you're so quick to hand it
to others.

Green Goddess

I am the earth goddess governed by the skies.
My growth progresses with each full moon.
The way in which my emotions ebb and flow.
I am the sap that resides in the trees.
I am the nectar that feeds the bees.
I am the raging river that brings you all your lost
hopes and dreams.
I am the wind that carries the seeds.
I am the leaves that get caught dancing in the
streets.

I am the branch that holds and houses God's creations.
I am the sun that delivers the very life force needed to maintain your spirit.
I am the grass beneath your feet, housing the energy released from your body.
I am the fallen tree who chooses to plant my roots and still rises to the occasion to meet the sun to hear the secrets it has to tell me.
I am the sun whispering to the tree to rise above its limitations and reach for the stars.
I am the sky that shows you there is no limit,
Your wishes are infinite.
The places you are so afraid to roam,
The next place could just be what you crave to call home.
Ever the last, just as the leaves, the trees, and the birds
I am the unspoken words of your soul you have yet to hear.
For you cannot be the caged bird who sings
Because you don't even know what it's like to let freedom ring.
How can you want someone to hear you speak,
When you don't even want to hear why the caged bird sings?
The bird does not sing for others' enjoyment,
But to be its own peace in times of distress.

I want you to hear the colors of this song, paint
the picture, and leave the rest.
There is no nest when all that you have left,
Are the places that your spirit has roamed,
Searching for a place to call home?
Finding solace in abandoned places where other
souls have laid down their burdens.
This is no place for me to call home, where other
souls have roamed, where their spirits have
occupied this space, a place where they no
longer belong.

Rooted

If men only understood women are like flowers.
A seed planted by God, to be surrounded by
darkness.
To allow earth to nourish her very being.
The rain that allows her very spirit to grow.
The sun that allows her feminine energy to
flourish and expand beyond the darkness.
Breaking through the barriers in which God has
planted her.
Allowing the sun to be the spotlight in which she
showcases her beauty.
Not for the mere gaze of men, but as a means to
thank nature.
For its nourishment, for its grounding, for the
space to grow and become the best version of
herself.
Now, you go into her field, picking the very
thing God planted.

Not for your enjoyment, but for you to
showcase.
Pruning her from the ground, admiring her
beauty at the moment the sun shines on her
silken petals.
You speak so highly of how she brightens up the
rooms in your home.
You make sure to water her, to place her by the
sunlight, to greet her just as the rising sun would
do each day.
Then one day you notice her petals are changing
colors, her leaves seem to be drying out.
"Add one food packet, change water daily or as
needed, keep out of direct sunlight," her
instructions read.
You walk past each day watching her wither
away.
Her petals no longer feel like silk, her leaves no
longer exude a bright green.
Signaling for the bees to land and rest their
bodies.
The bees…
The very reason she was surrounded by not only
the dirt, the sun, the rain…
But the beauty that lay among her.
It was the bees who ensured she stood tall.
It was the bees who stopped to sit and talk with
her.

It was the bees who greeted her with their gentle buzz in passing.

You see, the moment you took her from the very things God provided to nourish her, you forgot the instructions he left for you.

Feed her, with words, with love, with attention, with kindness.

Change her water daily. What she loved 3 days ago may not apply today.

So be sure to check and see if anything has changed.

Keep out of direct sunlight. Just as God buried her.

She opened herself to the sun when needed, and her petals retreated when she needed rest.

You ensured she stayed "fed" long enough that she met the standards you set.

But did you ever stop to ask God if you were ready to give her the love and care she needed?

If you were ready to provide what was required of you?

Next time, may the flowers you meet greet you with a smile.

May their bright colors paint a picture within the walls of your mind.

Just so you can be reminded that beauty is in the eye of the beholder.

Not confined within the walls of your home.

Letter To My Inner Child

Use your voice. Everyone isn't going to be accepting of you, your voice, or how you feel. Don't create to be chosen but for the sake of passion. Passion, that ever-burning fire no one can blow out. You cannot force yourself to move at the pace everyone wants you to. You cannot force yourself to move at the pace you want to. Slow down; there is beauty in the slow lane. Think of all the things you may have missed cause you were playing catch-up with everyone else. Do what you want for YOU! Do you wanna put out amazing products? Do you want to write a storybook status, even if people don't read it? Stop living your life for other people and do the things you want to do for you. It's okay if no one cares, it's okay if people prefer someone else over you. Everyone won't like you. A lot of people may feel like you're too much, or a lot to handle. Don't dim your light. There is and always will be someone out there who appreciates how brightly you shine. Even the way you shine light in their darkest corners. Not everyone is ready to feel the intensity of what it means to be human. That doesn't mean you stop living. Continue to create a life that you can be happy with, when, and if you are ready to share that. For right now, it's okay to feel and be different.

50 Shades of Love

I didn't know where this love would take me. It was the kind of thing they only spoke about in movies. Worshipping the ground that I walk on and wanting to cater to my every need. Kissing my feet after a hard day and wanting to hear about the details that sewed the seeds leaving me throwing my head over the seat, seeking even just an ounce of relief. The smile that sat upon your face because you're so happy to see me. You know, just as well as I, this was a love you weren't looking for, but it came anyway. As I sat there I began to stumble upon my words, falling into a deep slumber. You kissed me one last time before covering me up. As soon as I woke up, I realized it was all a dream. It was simply another vision of what's to come. The smell of your cologne, the taste of blueberry pie on your lips. All that seemed to fade as I realized where I was. It was those random moments that I caught a glimpse of who you are, whom I have yet to meet. As I sat there, I have seen your ring finger tapping on the glass. It seems, just as I did, this was a love you weren't ready to let go of. You proceeded, sat, and sulked over what could've been. You drowned your sorrows in what seemed like your umpteenth glass. Until you realized it was time to go home. You reminisce and replay giving your children a kiss before bedtime. Knowing it's a possibility that won't be your nightly routine anymore. So now you just fill your cup to forget the memories. Releasing what's no longer your normal. You ask, what do I do with myself? You contemplate, should I take on a hobby? Should I go back to school? This is probably your 5th time at the bar this week. The bartender is under the impression you're just having a fight with your wife. Go home, Christian. Go home to that beautiful wife and kids of yours. Your eyes glazed looking into the glass of whiskey; you whisper, I can't. I just can't. Only you know why. You know one day you'll have to face the music and finish packing. Realizing the house you reside in is no longer a home.

I Am

I am worth more than the intoxicating words that
fall from my lips.
I am more than the curves of my God-given
hips.
As they move to a rhythm so sweet and slow,
bringing you to the climax of your life, releasing
all your pain and inhibitions within me. Just for
me to take home and nurture.
I am more than just a woman that produces.
For I bear legacies within my womb to carry on
the knowledge of your seed that you have
planted within me.
I am more than the extensions of beauty for what
they call hair. As I walk beside you like a trophy
wife. Just for you to size me up and stare.

I am more than the nurturer you make me out to
be. Subconsciously nursing the wounds that
came from the womb of a woman who birthed
you.
I am more than a church wife. For I bear a magic
so powerful within me that my ancestors rise in
joy at the curses I have stood forth in the storm
to break. The greatness I have manifested with
the gifts that have passed onto me to heal our
lineage.
I am more than the woman you knew two years
ago, for I too have died and birthed a new legacy
to carry on what will now be my family tree.
I am a Goddess; allow me to reintroduce myself
as I step into all the glory that was bestowed
upon me as I rose from the ashes of what was
meant to break me.

Pretty Eyes

Pretty eyes, you don't realize, the beauty that lies within you. The unspoken words that fall from your lips as your cheeks rise and your lips widen to show that beautiful smile. Pretty eyes, you don't realize, that when you light up my world, it makes my heart smile. The way it flutters is that of a butterfly, preparing for its next destination as it begins to fly. Pretty eyes, you don't realize, how much you've been a blessing in disguise to me. Things, the things in my life that no longer served me, hurt me, didn't love me the way I deserved to be. Pretty eyes, you don't realize, the amount of joy you've brought me. For I thought the stork was only bringing me a bundle of joy. Only to my surprise, it was my literal saving grace. Pretty eyes, you don't realize, the tears I have cried. Wiping away the part of the time that I once despised. Only to see a part of me I never knew possible. Pretty eyes, I now realize, that only God could've brought me a literal Angel to show me the light I didn't know I needed. One as bright as your smile, as the lights beaming from your eyes. Pretty brown eyes, don't forget, you're more than meets the eye.

Pressure

Your hands sinking into my skin,
gliding across each curve like freshly sharpened
blades on ice.
Your fingertips sensing every crease and crevice.
Melting away the pressure that
lies beneath.
The heat emanating from your hands,
probing for areas that need relief.
Oil gliding from my legs up to my thighs.
Your arms pressing against my body, as though
you're seeking to release the secrets it holds.
Raising to your will, stretching and folding,
bending and pulling.
My body relinquishes itself to you.